Sports Fishing in Thailand

Arthur Crandon LL.B. (Hons.) M.A.

Sports Fishing in Thailand

Copyright Arthur Crandon 2024

All rights reserved. No part of this book may be reproduced, stored in a retrieval system, or transmitted in any form or by any means—electronic, mechanical, photocopying, recording, or otherwise—without the prior written permission of the publisher, except for brief quotations in critical reviews or articles.

This is a work of fiction. Names, characters, places, and incidents are either the product of the author's imagination or used fictitiously.. Any resemblance to actual persons, living or dead, events, or locales is entirely coincidental.

ISBN: 9798340001412

Cover design by Lance Ceniza

Interior design and formatting by Lynnie Ceniza

Published by Arthur Crandon Publishing

Visit our website: Arthurcrandon.co.uk

DISCLAIMER

The information provided in this book is for general informational purposes only. It does not constitute legal, financial, or professional advice. While every effort has been made to ensure accuracy, the author and publisher assume no responsibility for errors or omissions. Readers should consult with appropriate professionals for specific advice tailored to their individual circumstances.

First Edition: Sept 2024

Thailand, with its stunning coastline, lush jungles, and diverse aquatic ecosystems, offers a paradise for sports fishing enthusiasts. Whether you're a seasoned angler or a beginner, there's something here for everyone. Let's dive into the opportunities, locations, and methods for sports fishing in Thailand

CONTENTS

1 Saltwater Fishing 1

2 Freshwater Fishing 5

3 Sustainable Fishing 9

4 Unique Species 13

5 Diversity 19

6 Shrimps and Bettas 23

7 Conservation 29

8 Top Fishing Locations 33

9 Cultural Significance 37

Thailand's aquatic ecosystems—rivers, lakes, and coastlines—are home to an incredible variety of fish species. From the vibrant coral reefs of the Andaman Sea to the murky waters of the Mekong River, each habitat hosts unique inhabitants.

1 SALTWATER FISHING

Thailand, with its stunning coastline, lush jungles, and diverse aquatic ecosystems, offers a paradise for sports fishing enthusiasts. Whether you're a seasoned angler or a beginner, there's something here for everyone. Let's dive into the opportunities, locations, and methods for sports fishing in Thailand:

Sports Fishing Opportunities in Thailand

1. Saltwater Fishing: The Andaman Sea and Gulf of Thailand

Thailand's natural position along the Andaman Sea and the Gulf of Thailand provides access to excellent saltwater fishing grounds. Here are some key opportunities:

- **Billfish**: Encounter the three fastest fish in the ocean—Sailfish, Black Marlin, and Blue Marlin. These powerful fighters offer blazing runs and acrobatic leaps. The prime season for Billfish runs from October to April, when the seas are more stable. The Andaman Sea (accessible from the west coast) is the hotspot for Billfish.

- **Wahoo and Mahi Mahi**: These sought-after pelagic species also roam Thailand's seas. Between the two, Wahoo are the better fighters. They're lightning-quick and capable of powerful, drag-screaming runs. Mahi Mahi are fun to wrestle as well, although they tire more quickly. Both species are delicious, making them popular catches in Thailand. You can find Wahoo and Mahi either in the Andaman Sea or in the country's namesake gulf.

In essence, as long as you can spend enough time on the water, you'll have the chance to catch Marlin, Sailfish, Wahoo, and Mahi Mahi almost wherever you start your journey from. So grab your gear, cast your line, and let the Thai waters weave their magic

2 FRESHWATER FISHING

Let's explore the exciting freshwater fishing opportunities in Thailand. Whether you're an avid angler or a curious beginner, Thailand's lakes and fishing parks offer a diverse range of experiences:

Freshwater Fishing in Thailand: Stocked Lakes and Hidden Gems

> **1. Predator Lakes: Gillhams and IT Lake**

- **Gillhams Fishing Resort**: Located in Krabi, Gillhams is a world-renowned fishing destination. Here, you'll encounter some of the toughest-fighting freshwater fish from around the globe. The stars of the show include:

  - **Arapaima**: These massive, prehistoric fish are native to South America but thrive in Thailand's warm waters. Arapaima can reach lengths of over 10 feet and put up an incredible fight.

  - **Redtail Catfish**: Known for their strength and stamina, Redtail Catfish are a favorite among anglers. They can grow to impressive sizes and test your skills.

  - **Giant Siamese Carp**: A true heavyweight, the Giant Siamese Carp is a prized catch. These carp can weigh over 100 pounds and provide an exhilarating battle.

- **IT Lake**: Located near Bangkok, IT Lake is another fantastic fishing park. It's stocked with a variety of species, including the ones mentioned above. The serene surroundings and well-maintained facilities make it a popular choice for anglers.

  ### 2. Jungle Fishing: Off the Beaten Path

- **Hidden Rivers and Jungle Streams**: If you're up for an adventure, explore Thailand's lush jungles. Jungle fishing allows you to connect with nature while targeting species like:

  - **Snakehead**: These aggressive predators thrive in freshwater habitats. Their ambush-style attacks and powerful strikes make them a thrilling catch.

  - **Featherback (Nile Tilapia)**: Known for their elongated bodies and distinctive dorsal fins, Featherback are challenging opponents.

3. Fly Fishing in Thailand

- **Fly Fishing Opportunities**: While not as common as other methods, some lakes in Thailand offer fly fishing experiences. Target species like:

  - **Pacu**: Resembling piranhas, Pacu are strong fighters. They inhabit freshwater lakes and rivers.

  - **Amazon Redtail Catfish**: These catfish are prized for their size and tenacity. Hooking one on a fly rod is an unforgettable experience.

Remember to respect local regulations, practice catch-and-release, and immerse yourself in the natural beauty of Thailand's freshwater ecosystems. Tight lines, and may your next catch be legendary!

3 SUSTAINABLE FISHING

Sustainable fishing practices and conservation are crucial for maintaining healthy marine ecosystems. Let's delve into some key aspects:

1. Catch and Release:

- When you catch a fish, consider releasing it back into the water. This practice helps maintain fish populations and ensures that future generations can enjoy fishing.

- Follow proper handling techniques to minimize stress on the fish during release.

2. **Respect Regulations:**

    o   Local fishing regulations exist for a reason—to protect fish stocks and maintain ecological balance.

    o   Be aware of size limits, closed seasons, and restricted areas. Compliance with these rules contributes to sustainable fishing.

3. **Reduce Plastic Pollution:**

    o   **Plastic pollution poses a significant threat to marine life.**

    Here's how you can help:

    - Minimize Single-Use Plastics: Avoid disposable plastic items like bags, bottles, and utensils.

    - Properly Dispose of Trash: Always dispose of your trash responsibly, especially when fishing near water bodies.

- Participate in Clean-Up Efforts: Join local beach or river clean-up initiatives to remove plastic waste from the environment.

Remember, every small action counts.

4 UNIQUE SPECIES

Let's dive deeper into the fascinating world of unique fish species found in Thailand's waters:

1. **Mekong Giant Catfish (Pangasianodon gigas)**:

   o The **Mekong giant catfish** is a true giant. Endemic to the Mekong River, it's one of Thailand's most spectacular fish. Here are some remarkable facts:

      ▪ **Size**: It shares the record for the largest freshwater fish in the world with the giant freshwater stingray. Some individuals can reach lengths

of over 10 feet and weigh several hundred pounds.

- **Teeth**: Interestingly, despite its massive size, the Mekong giant catfish has no teeth in adulthood.

- **Conservation Status**: Unfortunately, this majestic fish is critically endangered due to factors like overfishing, habitat destruction, and dam construction along the Mekong River.

2. **Climbing Perch (Anabas testudineus)**:

    o Also known as the **"Walking Fish,"** the climbing perch is a common inhabitant of Thailand's lakes, rivers, and swamps. Here's what makes it unique.

- **Adaptation**: The climbing perch has an accessory air-breathing organ, allowing it to survive out of water for days. It can "walk" using its fins on dry land—an impressive adaptation.

3. **Alligator Gar (Atractosteus spatula)**:

   o Although not native to Thailand, the **alligator gar** was introduced by sport fishers from the USA. Here's what sets it apart:

    - **Appearance**: Its alligator-like snout and teeth give it a distinctive look.

    - **Habitat**: It inhabits freshwater pools, swamps, and bayous.

4. **Giant Snakehead (Channa micropeltes)**:

- The **giant snakehead** is a predatory freshwater fish found in Thailand's Mekong and Chao Phraya basins. What makes it special?

    - **Name**: Its elongated body and snakish head give it its intriguing name.

    - **Habitat**: It prefers slow-moving or standing bodies of water and is a prized catch for anglers.

5. **Cave-Dwelling Fish Species**:

    - Thailand hosts unique cave-dwelling fish species, adapted to life in darkness. These include:

        - **Cave Sheatfish**: Found in subterranean environments.

        - **Blind Cave Loach**: A fascinating adaptation to the absence of light.

- **Cave Angel Fish**: An endemic genus found nowhere else but in Thailand's caves.

These remarkable fish contribute to Thailand's rich biodiversity and offer a glimpse into the intricate web of life within its waters.

5 DIVERSITY

Let's dive deeper into the fascinating world of **Thailand's fishes**, exploring their diversity, conservation efforts, and cultural significance:

Exploring the Rich Fishes of Thailand: Diversity, Conservation, and Cultural Significance

1. Diversity of Fishes in Thailand

Thailand's aquatic ecosystems—rivers, lakes, and coastlines—are teeming with an incredible variety of fish species. From the smallest freshwater inhabitants to the majestic giants of the ocean, Thailand's waters offer a rich tapestry of marine and freshwater habitats.

Here are some highlights:

- **Whale Shark**: The gentle giant of the ocean, the **Whale Shark**, occasionally graces Thailand's waters. These filter-feeding behemoths play a crucial role in maintaining marine balance.

- **Siamese Fighting Fish (Betta splendens)**: Known for their vibrant colors and territorial behavior, Siamese fighting fish are not only popular in aquariums but also hold cultural significance.

2. Conservation Efforts in Thailand

- **Protected Areas**: Thailand has established marine and freshwater protected areas to safeguard critical habitats. These areas serve as sanctuaries for endangered species.

- **Breeding Programs**: Initiatives focus on

breeding and releasing endangered fish species back into the wild. The **Giant Mekong Catfish**, once on the brink of extinction, benefits from such programs.

- **Regulations and Licensing**: Thailand has shifted from an "open access" system to a controlled licensing regime. Scientific evidence guides maximum sustainable yield (MSY) and total allowable catch to prevent overexploitation.

Thailand's waters are not only a treasure trove of biodiversity but also a reflection of its cultural heritage. Whether it's the majestic Whale Shark or the tiny Siamese fighting fish, each species has a story to tell. Let's celebrate and protect these underwater wonders!

6 SHRIMP AND BETTAS

Let's dive into Thailand's fascinating role in aquaculture and explore the world of ornamental fish, particularly the captivating bettas (Siamese fighting fish).

Shrimp Production and Exports in Thailand

1. **Shrimp Farming Restoration Plan:** Thailand has long been a global leader in shrimp production and exports. However, in recent years, challenges such as disease epidemics, rising production

costs, and the impact of the COVID-19 pandemic led to a decline in marine shrimp

production. To address this, the Thai government initiated the **Thai Marine Shrimp Farming Restoration Plan (2022-2023)**.

2. The goal is to increase marine shrimp production to **400,000 tons by 2023**. The plan emphasizes disease control, quality, safety, and environmentally friendly practices that meet international standards. Key approaches include spatial management, collaboration among agencies, knowledge sharing, and the use of biosafety systems.

3. **Impressive Export Figures:** Thailand's prowess in shrimp exports is remarkable. In 2023, the total export value of shrimp products from Thailand amounted to approximately **42.37 billion Thai baht**. These exports

include various forms of shrimp, such as chilled and frozen shrimps, steamed and boiled shrimps, dried shrimps, canned shrimps, and seasoned and preserved shrimps. Additionally, the export volume reached around **137,300 tons** in the same year.

Siamese Fighting Fish (Bettas)

Now, let's turn our attention to the captivating world of ornamental fish, specifically the Siamese fighting fish, commonly known as bettas:

1. **Origins and Selective Breeding:**

   o Betta fish (scientifically known as *Betta splendens*) are native to Southeast Asia, including Thailand. Their natural habitats include rice paddies, slow-moving streams, and floodplains.

   o Through years of selective breeding, Thai enthusiasts have transformed wild bettas into living works of art. These fish are renowned for their vibrant colors and flowing fins.

- The global popularity of bettas has made them a source of immense pride for the Thai people, and they are considered a national icon.

2. **Varieties of Bettas:**

    - **Pla Kat Luk Moh:** These bettas have thick trunks, large heads, and dark fins. They come in various colors, including red, dark blue, purple, green, and copper. Known for their tenacity, they are favored for sparring.

    - **Pla Kat Luk Toong:** Smaller but longer, these bettas have long red fins with green tints. They are swift but have poor stamina.

    - **Hybrid Betta (Pla Kat Luk Pasom):** Spawned by cross-breeding, these hybrids combine the best traits of Luk Moh and Luk Toong. They have better endurance.

- **Pla Kat Jeen:** Bred for aesthetics, these bettas have long fins and vivid colors. They move gracefully, reminiscent of Chinese opera performers.

3. **Warrior Instincts and Competitions:**

    - Betta fish are known for their warrior instincts, high endurance, and readiness to attack. Thais have enjoyed betta-fighting competitions since ancient times.

    - Villagers gather after work for thrilling matches, showcasing their prized bettas' strength and agility.

4. **National Aquatic Animal:**

    - The Siamese fighting fish holds a special place in Thai culture. It was declared Thailand's **National Aquatic Animal** in 2019.

So, whether it's shrimp farming or the mesmerizing bettas, Thailand's aquatic contributions are both practical and enchanting!

7 CONSERVATION

Let's delve deeper into Thailand's remarkable conservation efforts and how they contribute to the protection of aquatic biodiversity:

1. Protected Areas:

- Thailand recognizes the critical importance of preserving its natural habitats. As a result, the country has established a network of marine and freshwater protected areas. These areas serve as havens for endangered species, allowing them to thrive without the pressures of human activity.

- **Within these protected zones, various ecosystems—from coral reefs to mangroves—are** safeguarded. For instance, Thailand's national marine parks, coastal non-hunting areas, and reserved mangrove forests play a vital role in maintaining biodiversity and supporting sustainable fisheries.

2. **Breeding Programs:**

    - To combat declining populations of endangered fish species, Thailand has implemented breeding programs. These initiatives focus on captive breeding and releasing fish back into their natural habitats.

    - One notable success story is the Giant Mekong Catfish (Pangasianodon gigas). Once critically endangered, this massive catfish now benefits from conservation efforts. By carefully managing breeding and reintroduction,

- Thailand aims to ensure the survival of this iconic species.

3. **Regulations and Licensing:**

    - In recent years, Thailand has undergone significant changes in its fisheries management. The new fisheries law shifted from an "open access" system to a controlled licensing regime.

    - Under this system, scientific evidence guides decisions related to maximum sustainable yield (MSY) and the total allowable catch (TAC). By setting sustainable limits on fishing, Thailand aims to prevent overexploitation and promote responsible practices.

    - This shift reflects a commitment to balancing economic interests with environmental conservation, ensuring that aquatic resources are managed for the long term.

Thailand's dedication to conservation, sustainable practices, and scientific management is commendable. By protecting its unique fish species and their habitats, Thailand contributes not only to its own biodiversity but also to the global effort to safeguard our oceans and aquatic ecosystems.

8 TOP FISHING LOCATIONS

Let's explore some of the top fishing locations in Thailand, each offering its own unique charm and exciting angling opportunities:

Phuket:

- **Marlin and Sailfish Paradise**: Phuket, Thailand's island paradise, is blessed with pristine beaches, turquoise waters, and incredible fishing opportunities. When you fish in Phuket, you'll have the chance to encounter some of the most sought-after species in the world.

- **Billfish**: Phuket's Andaman Sea is home to big game species like Sailfish, Black Marlin, and Blue Marlin. These fish put up unmatched fights, with blazing runs and acrobatic leaps. The prime season for Billfish is from October to April, when the seas are more stable and offshore outings are ideal.

- **Wahoo and Mahi Mahi**: These pelagic species also roam Phuket's waters. Wahoo are lightning-quick fighters, while Mahi Mahi combine fun wrestling with delicious taste.

- **Snapper and Grouper**: Bottom fishing around reefs, wrecks, and rock formations yields Snapper and Grouper. The Racha Islands and the drop-off are popular spots for these catches from October to April.

2. **Khao Lak**:

    o **Prime Fishing During Dry Season**: Khao Lak, known for its pristine beaches, is a fantastic fishing destination. The dry season extends from November to April, offering high temperatures and calm seas.

    o **Localized Weather**: Khao Lak's unique geographic location means that weather can change rapidly. However, it's generally warm year-round.

    o **Snorkeling and Diving**: Khao Lak's calm and clear waters during the dry season make it perfect for snorkeling and diving trips to the Similan or Surin Islands.

3. **Similan Islands**:

    o **Snorkeling and Fishing Paradise**: The Similan Islands, located in the Andaman Sea, are famous for their top scuba diving spots and pristine beaches.

- Snorkeling here is fantastic, with abundant shallow reefs.

- **Snorkeling Daytrips**: Explore the islands via snorkeling day trips. Speedboats take you to the best spots, where you'll swim with sea turtles and colorful fish.

- **Jigging and Popper Fishing**: For anglers, the Similan Islands offer opportunities to catch Amberjack, Tuna, Spanish mackerel, Wahoo, Barracuda, and more.

Whether you're battling Billfish offshore, exploring tranquil lakes, or combining snorkeling with fishing, Thailand's fishing scene promises unforgettable experiences. Tight lines, and may your next catch be legendary!

9 CULTURAL SIGNIFICANCE

Fish hold profound cultural significance in Thailand, woven into the fabric of daily life, traditions, and spirituality. Let's explore how fish are revered and cherished in Thai culture:

1. Abundance and Fertility:

- In Thai culture, fish symbolize abundance and fertility. They are more than just a source of sustenance; they represent prosperity and well-being.

- An ancient inscription attributed to King Ramkhamhaeng the Great, ruler of the Sukhothai Kingdom, describes a thriving land with fish in the water and rice in the fields. This portrayal emphasizes the importance of fish as a symbol of settled civilization and prosperity.

- When people were too poor to afford fish, they would hang small model cut-outs of fish in their homes while eating their bowls of rice—a symbolic gesture of abundance and hope.

2. **Spiritual Cleansing and Renewal:**

- The Traditional Thai Songkran Festival, which marks the Thai New Year, highlights the significance of water. Water is used for purification, renewal, and washing away sins.

- During Songkran, people splash water on each other, cleansing themselves of negative energy and starting the new year afresh. Pouring water over Buddha statues is also a respectful ritual, symbolizing gratitude and blessings for the year ahead.

3. Thai Culinary Traditions Involving Fish:

- **Thai cuisine celebrates fish in various delectable dishes:**

    - Pla Thot (Deep-Fried Fish): Fish, such as catfish, mackerel, or snapper, is fried to crispy perfection, often with head, fins, bones, and tail intact. It's both a culinary delight and a cultural tradition.

    - Pla Neung Manao (Steamed Fish with Lime Garlic Sauce): Barramundi fish is steamed with lemongrass, lime juice, garlic, and other flavorful ingredients. The sauce is poured over the fish, creating a harmonious blend of flavors.

- Pla Sam Rot (Three-Flavor Fish): Sea bass, tilapia, or snapper is fried and topped with a sauce combining tamarind (sour), palm sugar (sweet), fish sauce (salty), and aromatic herbs. It's traditionally served as a shared meal with steamed jasmine rice.

4. **Conservation Efforts:**

   o Thailand actively participates in ocean conservation projects. Initiatives like the Phuket Save the Sea Project organize underwater clean-up dives to remove litter from the ocean, protecting marine life.

   o Leatherback turtles, an endangered species, have returned to nest on Kata Beach in Phuket due to conservation efforts and calmer beach atmospheres.

In summary, fish are not only a culinary delight but also a cultural treasure in Thailand. Let's continue to celebrate and protect these underwater wonders!

Visit Arthurcrandon.co.uk for More Titles

Retirement to the Philippines
K1 Fiance visa to the U.S. – Fast Track
Secrets to buying Condos in the Philippines
Buying Land in the Philippines
Annulment in the Philippines
Breaking free from a bad marriage
Get a visit visa to America First time
Marriage in the Philippines
Get a visit visa to the United Kingdom
Ghosts, Spectres, and folklore in the Philippines
Retiring to Spain – a Comprehensive Guide
Spousal Visa to America
Spousal visa to the United Kingdom
Working in the UK.
Working in the US.

ABOUT THE AUTHOR

Arthur Crandon is a retired lawyer and a prolific writer. He is British and grew up in a rural community in Somerset. He has lived in England, Wales, Hong Kong and the Philippines and now spends most of his time in the Philippines with his Visayan wife and their son.

He loves to hear from anyone who has anything to do with the Philippines – you can email him anytime on:

ac@arthurcrandon.co.uk

Printed in Great Britain
by Amazon